Human

Behavior

Owino Peter Kennedy

ISBN-13: 978-1534806986
ISBN-10: 1534806989

DEDICATION

This is a special dedication to Br Raymond Kuzoch of the Congregation of the Priests of the Sacred Heart. May God bless you always in your service.

CONTENTS

ACKNOWLEDGMENTS

I do acknowledge the great contribution of my tutors in different institutions together with those who have journeyed with me. Receive much embrace as you get the opportunity to understand this work which majorly talks about human behaviors.

Remain blessed.

Introduction

In our times the aggressive behaviors of the individual is greatly misunderstood. On the one hand, social evils such as war and crime have been blamed on aggression or even called aggression, as if the participants in these destructive social phenomena were acting out of misdirected individual aggressive behavior. On the other hand, the positive role of anger in the activists who tried to change society in order to eliminate these evils has been ignored and even suppressed.

Aggression is an appropriate topic for social psychology because it always involves two people-a victim and an aggressor. AGGRESSION is defined as any behavior that is intended to hurt another living being . VIOLENCE refers to extreme acts of physical aggression. Note that intention to hurt is a key component of aggression. By this definition, accidental injury is not an aggressive act. It is useful to differentiate hostile aggression and instrumental aggression. Instrumental aggression is a behavior that is intended to hurt another living being, but where the aggression is motivated to achieve a goal. An example is a football player who intentionally hurts an opponent in order to gain an advantage on the field and win the game. By contrast, hostile aggression is solely intended to cause harm-for instance, a husband punching his wife during a heated argument .

What causes aggressive behavior? Is aggression innate and unavoidable, or is it learned through experiences and therefore potentially preventable? At present, there is no unified theory of human aggression. However, over 100 years of research have produced some clear findings. At present social psychologists have a good understanding of many factors that contribute to aggressive behavior and can predict with considerable accuracy who is likely to act aggressively and the situations that are likely to produce these behaviors.

Most people will agree that aggression can become dangerous and that is a serious problem. The source of different acts of aggression is trying to be understood from medical, psychological and cultural perspectives. Some scientists tried to treat the abnormal aggressive behavior with medication, while others go deeper and try to find out why they have abnormal behavior. Some answers are biological, like genes and hormones, other answers are psychological, like rejection as a cause of aggression, and still others are cultural, blaming aggression on violence in the media.

Sometimes it feels as if the society we live in has turned painfully aggressive; an aggressive world in which everything seems to be in competition against each other, from the animal kingdoms 'fight for the survival to the different governments', fight for domination/leadership and the resources of this planet. On an individual level, all our senses are being constantly bombard with a flood of emotions, such as fear, hatred, pain, enviousness and many more which all have one main outcome in common; aggression. An aggression so intense that it boils the blood that pulsates through our veins, it causes inner turmoil and makes us do things we would have never done. In short it turns us into animalistic zombies.

This book is composed of four sections or simply chapters, and in all these chapters I have tried briefly to come up with the research findings of psychology on Human aggression. In chapter one, is all about the history of human aggression starting from the ancient time to the current situation. I have elaborated how humanity perceived aggression in their lives from the past centuries and how they treated each other.

In the second chapter is all about some of the African tribes, how aggression is seen in their tribes, of course African tribes are being regarded as warriors like people but what is the degree of their actions? I came up with some of the psychological analysis on African tribes as well as development and understanding of aggression in Africa.

The last two chapters are all about the nature and causes of aggression as well as the controlling of aggression. Therefore it is in these two chapters that I have given up some of the theories of aggression which have been proposed by social psychologists.

CHAPTER ONE

AGGRESSION IN HUMAN HISTORY

1.1. Origins of Aggression

A popular evolutionary explanation of aggression is the 'best within' view. According to this view, "survival of the fittest" has bred aggression in human beings. It is thus 'human nature' to be aggressive. Modern evolutionary psychology has a more sophisticated view. This view states that 'human nature' includes a lot of psychological mechanisms and motives. Men are more physically and verbally aggressive than women. Aggression is just one technique among many others that humans use as they strive for mastery as material resources, as well as for respect from and connectedness to others.

1.1.1.   Is Aggression innate?

One way to determine if aggression is an innate human trait is to examine other cultures. If just one culture can be found that values cooperation and nurturing over violence, then we can conclude that aggression is a learned cultural response, not a human instinct. And in fact a whole spectrum of aggression levels can be found in pre-literate cultures. Some are extremely violent warrior's societies where aggression is highly valued. But other cultures are gentle and peaceful, with few of violent crime or war.

We are not "hard-wired" like bugs or ducks, where a given stimulus results in a fixed response. Unlike most animals, we have a large cerebral cortex that allows for reasoning, consideration, creativity and culture.

The instinct controlling part of our brain is relatively insignificant in comparison to the cortex and can be superseded by will and thought. It is this "flexible response" capability that enables human to survive and rise above the rest of the animal kingdom. Many anthropologists feel it was our ability to cooperate, not our ability to fight (compete), that was our evolutionary survival trait.

Because of our ability to reflect and continuously choose the values we still in our children, as a species we can be whatever we want to be. It can almost be sat that there is no such thing as human nature, that almost all our traits and tendencies are culturally defined. This is not as obvious as it should be, because most of us are only exposed to one culture (a culture where everyone pretty much thinks and acts the same) and it's easy to get the impression that the way we are is the only way we can be. It is not instinct that drives us to commit atrocities, but our culture. Culture is a human creation. Our culture was modeled by men who crave power and the domination of others.

1.1.2. Is aggression learned?

Albert Bandura believed that aggression is learned through a process called behavior modeling. He believed that individuals do not actually inherit violent tendencies, but they modeled them after three principles. Albert Bandura argued that individuals, especially children learn aggressive responses from observing others, either personally or through the media and environment. He stated that many individuals believed that aggression will produce reinforcements. These reinforcements can formulate into reduction of tension, gaining financial rewards, or gaining the praise of others, or building self-esteem. There are different reasons why a person may act aggressively towards other human beings. The person may act this way because of his culture or the way he was brought up in the society. The person does not, however acts this way based on instinct alone. Aggression is a molded learned behavior. A human being must have both environmental and instinctual factors in order to display aggression. Some of person's natural instincts are to desire food, reject certain things, escape from change, fight when challenged, sex desire, care for the young and the likes. The combination of instincts and environment determines a person's behavior. This is based on the theory that everything human being would do have to be learned from other human beings. Aggression must be learned; it is not simply there from birth. Rather than being an uncontrollable instinct, a person's behavior is something that is taught to him. For example a newborn baby is breathing because it is an involuntary reflex. On the other hand, a father may tell his young son to beat up the bully who is picking up on him.

1.2. Aggression in the ancient time

When we think of the prehistoric times, we may picture a word similar to that of the Flintstones, granted not as a fanciful or whimsical. However, this notion of the caveman, of a brutish hulk of an organism that was strong as rock and about half intelligent is not too far from the truth. Though time and pop culture may have skewed what the common person may know about our prehistoric ancestors. The essentials are there: they were a primitive species ruled by instinct, specifically aggression. Aggression was a necessity to survive in the time before human civilization, i.e. "survival of the fittest". Aggressiveness was a trait that aided our ancestors to ward of predators, amass food, and attract mates so that their genes would be passed on. In archeological digs, prehistoric corpses have traces of severe wounds that the body sustained while alive,

indicating signs of interpersonal aggression amongst primitive cultures.
As man crept out from the murky depths of the prehistoric era and set
forth to build the basis of future civilizations, he brought with him his
violent and aggressive tendencies. Sparta, the Trojan war, Sargon the
Great, the Assyrian Empire and their brutal successors of the
Babylonians and Egyptians, and many more examples give but a mere
glimpse into the aggressiveness of ancient people. Even culturally man
was highly influenced by aggression, as seen in the Bible and depictions
of God's divine wrath upon his enemies.

1.2.1.   Account of aggression in the book of Genesis

The story of Cain and Abel, written in the Torah and the Bible at Genesis
4, and Qur'an at 5:27-32, tells of the first human murder when Cain
killed his brother Abel. They were the sons of Adam and Eve and the
murder a result of their fall. Many religious faiths view this as the
prototypical murder and paradigm for conflict and violence. While some
view this story as merely a story of the origin of humanity, and others as
a justification of murder, it is generally interpreted as a tragedy in human
relationships. Cain and Abel represent different personality types or
social positions. Cain represents the firstborn, sinful, worldly, privileged,
a farmer, a city builder and bad son. Abel represents the junior, faithful,
spiritual, herdsman and good son.

The Cain and Abel story is set in the Ancient Near East about 6,000
years ago. Many modern scholars believe the biblical account derives
from earlier stories of conflict between the traditional nomadic way of
life of the Israelites and the agricultural way of life which was
developing in the fertile resent.

Christian theology derived from St Augustine sees a constant separation of Cain and Abel, the former destined for hell and latter bound for heaven. Social psychologists would view Cain's action as an example of the frustration-aggression hypothesis and advocate teaching non-violent responses to frustration. In basic disagreement with the Augustinian view, many today argue that God equally loves both sons and desires the reconciliation of Cain and Abel as the brothers they are. Successful strategies for the resolution of Cain-Abel conflicts can be seen as a paradigm for conflict resolution generally.

1.3. Aggression in the middle ages

1.3.1. The Crusades

The crusades were a series defensive war against Islamic aggression in the middle ages and attempts to recapture the Holy Land from Muslim conquerors in order to allow safe pilgrimage and to maintain the Christian presence there. Jerusalem had been Christian for hundreds of years when Caliph Omar seized it, and following that victory, Muslims warred way into Egypt, other parts of Africa, Spain, Sicily and Greece, leaving Christians dead and churches in ruins. They stole lands in the area now known as Turkey, destroying Catholic communities founded by St. Paul himself. They seized Constantinople the "second Rome"… and threatened the Balkans.

In contrast, the crusades had profound and lasting effect on medieval Europe. Form the Christian perspective until recent times, the crusades were seen as liberation, not aggression. The crusades initially elevated the authority of the papacy as the authoritative spiritual and temporal power in Europe prior to the emergence of nation-states. Yet with the decent of the crusades into indiscriminate slaughter of innocents and aggression against fellow Christians, the moral authority of the papacy and unity of Christendom in Europe suffered.

In the twentieth century, the term "crusades" was revived by some Muslims as a description of what they regard as a Christian-Jewish campaign to destroy the Muslim world. Attacks on Muslim states by majority Christian western powers in the early twenty-first century have been compared to the crusades. Both are depicted as wars of aggression.

1.3.2. The medieval era

As the church moved beyond the early centuries into the era of the medieval world, several things began to change, both in the world and in the church.

Evangelicals often think of the medieval era as a time of spiritual across much of Europe. It is thought that the church was cold, lifeless, and dead. That the true story is quite different surprises such people.

In the early centuries the church was a persecuted minority, by the time it entered the medieval world it was an aggressive component of the establishment. This shift had begun with the conversion of Emperor Constantine in the early fourth century, by the eighth and night centuries, the church had won its battles with pagan cultures, and its thought and life became associated with the cause of victory. Triumph brought with it a distinct theological emphasis upon the language of victory over the devil, sin and death! It also brought the related problems of ecclesiastical triumphalism, a kind of celebrative spirit connected with victory over others.

As the old Roman Empire broke up and more familial ways of thinking and living developed in Europe, people became concerned about right thinking regarding their personal relationship to God and to the church. As surely as the doctrines of God, Christ, man and sin had occupied the attention of the early centuries, so now the church would address in a more focused way the doctrine of salvation. How was the great disruption between man and God to be resolved? How do I enter into fellowship with an offended, holy God?

1.4. Aggression in modern time

For as far back as we have recorded history, wars have been waged in order for territorial gain or in order to conquer another nation. The concept that the stronger nation should prevail was largely accepted throughout the world until the 20th century, when the concept of aggression without justification began to lose favor. A new term-"war of aggression"- began to make its way into the nomenclature of many languages as a way to describe a war that serves no justifiable purpose, such as self-defense. Since then the world view of aggression has changed to the point that crimes of aggression are now considered international right along with human trafficking and genocide.

When one nation or a faction thereof, engages in armed conflict against another nation without provocation, it is said to have waged a war of aggression. In modern times, a war of aggression is considered unacceptable among nations of the world. Although the precise definition of a war of aggression may be disputed, most scholars agree that a war without the justification of self-defense sits the definition.

1.4.1. The colonization

Between the 1870s, Africa faced European imperialist aggression, diplomatic pressures, military invasions, and eventual conquest and colonization. At the same time, African societies put up various forms of resistance against the attempt to colonize their countries and impose foreign domination. By early twentieth century, however, much of Africa, except Ethiopia and Liberia had been colonized by European powers.

Oppression is a basic ingredient of colonialism. There is no denying if that oppression dehumanizes both the oppressor and the oppressed. Thus in the thickness of colonialism, national movements, and most of them were radical and violent in their approaches, emerged to encounter the aggression of colonialism. The natives after some period of submission, due to changes in world ideologies and political climate realized that the settler are mere drones living off blood and labor of the native without awarding him his dues. The natives realized that his hopes and aspirations would remain stifled under the rule of the colonizer. Thus the native resorted to violence to shake the colonizer off his shoulder and eventually he did.

1.5. Aggression in the contemporary time

1.5.1. Economical

The ministerial forum on China-Africa cooperation met in Sharm el-sheik, Egypt, attended by Chinese premier Wen Jiabao and representatives of more than 300 Chinese companies. Wen took the opportunity to chide the US for its large budget deficit. He made clear that China intended to press ahead its program of investment in Africa despite American opposition. He pledged $ 10 billion in concessional loans with lower interest rates and longer repayment periods than standard loans to Africa over the next three years. His offer was mainly welcomed by African ministers.

Within days of the conference closing, the US responded. The International monetary fund threatened to cut off lines of credit to the Democratic Republic of Congo if it did not scale back a Chinese investment plan. The IMF, a body dominated by the US, showed that it is quite prepared to plunge this war-torn and improvised African country into financial isolation, a fate that has already befallen Zimbabwe, with disastrous consequences for the mass population.

1.5.2. Terrorism

According to Wikipedia, the word " terrorism" has over 100 meanings, and currently has no universally agreed upon, legally binding, criminal law definition. This is unfortunate, but most understand the real meaning whether they choose to apply it properly or not. The word "terror" comes from the Latin verb *terrere* meaning to be frantic with fear or terror. Generally speaking, terrorism is the use of violence or threats to intimidate or coerce, especially for political purposes. It is violent acts intended to create fear, and these acts are perpetrated for a religious, political or ideological goal, and deliberately target or disregard the safety of civilians.

The United States government, and those in the US military who willingly do the bidding of the government by prosecuting immoral and aggressive wars and acts hostility, and those who are partners in these crimes, are the worst terrorist in the world today.

Without question, the worst single terrorist act in the United States history was the attack that took place on September 11, 2001. On that horrible day 2,996 people were killed, and many others wounded. It was truly awful and was purposely meant to harm innocent. If one goes to the Wikipedia and does a little research to find out what are supposed to be the worst terrorist attacks in history, the worst event listed since 1940s is 9/11. But it is important to understand that the nuclear bombs purposely dropped on civilian centres in Hiroshima and Nagasaki in WWII.

1.6. Aggression in the Religious perspective

Religion has often been a tool for those aggressive tendencies. The positive aspects of the religious inclination, including compassion, and altruism, are often limited to a religious in-group. While the predominate activity is aggression toward those with different beliefs and values. Fundamentalist religions appear to be a manifestation of the authoritarian personality.

The concept of "religious war" is one of the more explicit manifestations of the instincts for aggression. The absurd contradiction between the core themes of spiritual teachings and the aggression of the religious groups is obvious to those outside of the group but not to those inside.

1.6.1. Christianity

Millions of Africans and Americans are Christians today because their ancestors were converted against their will to the religion of the slave-master. Hundreds of thousands of Americans and Indians are Christians today because Christian missionaries converted their ancestors against their will.

In Europe, it was the same thing. When Rome controlled most of the world, the Roman Emperor, Constantine, in 325CE forced Christianity into his subjects. The people of Lithuania did not become Christians because they read the Gospel and decided to accept their teachings. On the contrary, the people of Lithuania were forced into Christianity against their will, as a result of relentless military force. From the crusades, by Bernard Hamilton:

"In 1309 the Teutonic order moved its headquarters to Marienburg in Prussia. It had a papal license to wage perpetual war against the pagans and used this to launch annual crusades against Lithuania. These expeditions were very popular the nobility of Northern Europe: campaigns were hold twice a year, in summer and in the winter when the order laid on special Christmas festivities for visiting crusaders".

The excuse for men who enjoyed fighting and to lay waste large parts of Lithuania in the name of Christ was removed in 1386 when the king of Lithuania, Ladislas Jagiello, married queen Jadwiga of Poland and received Catholic baptism. The two kingdoms were united under Christian rulers and the Teutonic knights no longer had any justification for crusading against pagans there.

Lithuania was not the first country that fell victim to a campaign of lethal military force, for the purpose of forced conversion to Christianity. Three entire European nationalities became victims of genocide because they refused to become Christians.

".. the Vandals, Ostrogoths, and the Heruli. The last three destroyed by the Pope of Rome because they refused to become 'christian'. The armies of Emperor Justinian, cooperation with the Pope, thrust the Ostrogoths out of the city of Rome. They have become extinct"

Christianity cannot take any pride for their large numbers of subjects. Almost all Christian ancestors, Catholics and Protestants really had to no choice in the matter. They were forced to accept Jesus as their Lord. Christianity was a forced religion. Today it is being in another manner, through an army of missionaries beating on your door.

1.6.2. Islamic

Today, there is a movement that claims 880 million followers worldwide; it is rapidly growing in Europe, Africa and America. This movement is very aggressive and often violent, teaching that if someone will not willingly convert that they must eventually eliminated. This movement boldly demand the death of all who would oppose it. The name of the movement is "Islam". It invaded the shores under the protection of religion, and is spreading in every direction. Islam however, is more than a religion: it is a comprehensive way of life. Those who defend Islam claim that Muslims desire to live peacefully with all men, yet facts of history proves that if and when Muslims gain control they will fight and even kill in order to eliminate all opposition to Islam.

The Quran and the Hadeeth, Muslim's holy books, contain the religious, social, civil, commercial, military, and legal codes for Muslims. What many people do not realize is that the teachings of Islam are not just ethical guidelines; they are binding laws with severe punishments attached to them that range from public whipping to chopping off of body parts and beheading. In the hands of extremists, this type of law once established inevitably leads to gross abuse and oppression. As in most countries where the Islamic code of law is enforced, the average citizens suffer while the crimes and hypocrisy of the wealthy and those in power go unpunished.

The most alarming thing about Islam is that if it becomes powerful enough, the option for those under its control wouldn't be whether to accept Islam or reject it. It would be, rather, whether to accept Islam or at best, become second class citizens, at worst face death.

CHAPTER TWO
HISTORY OF AGGRESSION IN AFRICA AND TRIBAL VARIATIONS

2.1. Traditional Africa and aggression

It is always helpful to approach the understanding of phenomenon by attempting to envisage its very beginning. When dealing with a phenomenon of human interaction this roundabout way may lead to important insights. But, when the origin apparently lies in the remotest past, we have to rely on imaginative reconstructions based on interpretations of available archaeological issues.

Retracing African's ancient stories is further complicated by a relative scarcity of archaeological data, and by prejudiced interpretation. Fortunately, however, ongoing investigations are dislodging mistaken assumptions, even the tenacious preconception that remarkable early achievements could not have been the work of Africans and have attributed to foreign skill. We therefore find ourselves at a juncture where several established ideas about hypothetical migrations, cultural labels and ethnic distinctions are being questioned and revised.

We can surely assume that earliest human inhabitants of Africa, just as human beings across the globe, experienced communicational difficulties and volitional differences. Misunderstanding could have happened mere frequently when languages were still in their rudimentary stages (although body language must have been as communicative as it is). Disagreement could have taken place very often, in spite of, precisely because of, attempts to instill conformity with traditions, decisions and behavior of the groups concerned. Greed could have been manifested whenever there was competition for a scarce resource, like food.

Seeing that these early communities were inevitably made up of the two genders, as well as of age sets, family clusters and ethnic groups, they could have experienced all sorts of relational problems. Out of incidents and attitudes of daily interaction prejudice and intolerance could have developed easily.

During the stages of human existence when the primary objectives were (initially) mere survival and (later) tribal strength, power began playing its never-ending role on the human scene. Almost always, however, power brings with it the misuse of power and, consequently also, various manifestations of injustice, domination and aggression. Although we have no means of proving it, we have every reason to suppose that these conflict-generating forces were already operative among the earliest people of Africa. If our early ancestors were as humanly human as we are, in spite of the great cultural differences between those ancient eras we and our present age, they must have experienced these same sources of inter human discord and conflict.

2.2. Aggression in modern Africa

While African resistance to European colonialism is often thought of in terms of a white and black/European and African power struggle, this presumption underestimates the complex and strategic thinking that Africans commonly employed to address the challenges of European colonial rule. It also neglects the colonial era power dynamic of which African societies and institutions were essential components.

After Berlin conference of 1884-85, at which the most powerful European countries agreed upon rules for laying claim to particular African territories, the British, French, Germans, Italians and the likes set about formally implementing strategies for the long-term occupation and control of Africa. The conquest had Berlin conference it became more systematic and overt.

The success of the European conquest and the nature of African resistance must be seen in light of Western Europe's long history of colonial rule and economic exploitation around the world. In fact, by 1885 western Europeans had mastered the art of divide, conquer, and rule, having their skills over four hundred years of imperialism and exploitation in the Americas, Asia, and the Pacific.

Europeans turned to Africa to satisfy their greed for resources, prestige, and empire, they quickly worked their way into African societies to gain allies and proxies, and to co-opt the conquered kings and chiefs, all to further their exploits. Consequently, the African responses to this process particularly the ways in which they resisted it, were complex. Adding to the complexity was the fact that rapid European imperial expansion did not necessarily change relationships among African communities. Those in conflict with one another tended to remain in conflict, despite the impending threat from the French, British, German, and other powers.

2.3. Understanding the development of aggression in Africa

Africa has a high prevalence of civil war and this is commonly attributed to the ethnic diversity of its countries. This inference seems self-evident to many, given that African rebel movements almost always are ethically defined. Ethnic identities and hatred are thus seen as the cause of violent conflict. However, more systematic analysis of the cause of civil war suggests that Africa's civil war was conform to a global pattern that is better explained by political and economic factors as well as by the extent of ethnic, cultural and religious in the society. Recent studies have found that the risk of civil war is reduced by the opportunity cost of rebel labor (proxy by indicators of economic development, such as per capita GDP or educational attainment)

Up to a certain range, natural resources are associated with higher risk of war, though for a substantial natural resources base the relationship is expected to turn negative. Natural resources provide easily "lootable" asserts for "loot-seeking" rebel movements or convenient sources of sustaining "justice seeking" movements. However, extremely plentiful resources may also provide sufficient revenues that the government can use to fund its army and "buy" popular support.

The literature of civil war also suggests that social diversity can have several offsetting effects that may reduce the risk of large-scale violent conflict. This may happen because rebel cohesion may be a function of the degree of ethnic or religious diversity of the society; in highly diverse societies, the government may be more easily successful in dividing the rebels given that the rebels themselves may have a harder time in gaining support for their cause access a wider range of ethnic groups with potentially diverse preferences. Collier and Hoeffler find that ethnic diversity becomes problematic when it borders polarization… i.e. when an ethnic group accounts for 60-40% of the population and can dominate the others. In such polarized societies, it is easier to start and support rebellion given the above analytical literature, two key questions with profound policy implications could be asked: what explains the high prevalence of civil wars in Africa? And how effective are economic development and political reforms in reducing the risk of civil wars?

2.4. Tribal variation of African tribes

2.4.1.   *Zulu*

The Zulu tribe is one of the Nguni/Ngoni people which is found in the Republic of South Africa, in the Kwazulu-natal province. It is one of the major tribe with the Xhosa. Historically speaking the Zulu people were considered as warriors being led by king Shaka, and it is where we find that their aggressive behavior is so dominant more especially towards their opponent, the Xhosa people. And from this point of view is where we find the Mfecane.

The word mfecane is derived from the Xhosa terms: ukufaca 'to become thin from hunger' and feteani 'starving intruders'. Mfecane refers to a period of political disruption and population migration in Southern Africa which occurred during the 1820. It is also known by the Sotho name Difeqane.

Euro-centric historians in the late nineteenth and early twentieth century's regarded the mfecane as the result of aggressive nation building by the Zulu under the rule of Shaka and the Ndebele under Mzilikazi. Such descriptions of devastation and depopulation of Africans gave white settlers an excuse for moving into the land which thus they considered empty.

By the 1960s the mfecane and Zulu nation building were being given a positive spin-considered more as a revolution in Bantu Africa, where Shaka played a leading role in the creation of a Zulu nation in natal, whilst Moshoeshoe similarly created the Sotho kingdom in what is now Lesotho as a defense against the Zulu incursions.

Modern historians challenge the suggestion that Zulu aggression caused the mfecane, citing archaeological evidence which shows that drought and environmental degradation lead to increased competition for land and water, which encouraged the migration of farmers and cattle herders throughout the region.

More extreme, and highly controversial, theories have been suggested, including the conspiracy theory that the myth of Zulu nation building and aggression was, a root cause of the mfecane was used to cover up systematic illegal slave trading by white settlers to feed the demand for labor in the cape colony and neighboring Portuguese Mozambique.

2.4.2.   Sotho

The Basotho nation was the work of a most unusual and gifted statesman. During the early years of the nineteenth century, Moshoeshoe, the young prince of an obscure Sotho section, began to take account of the defensive possibilities of the flat-topped hills which were common to the mountainous region just west of the Drankensberg scarp opposite Natal. He saw that the heights could be defended against large numbers of attackers if properly provisioned and fortified. With a small group of young men he therefore established himself on an upland called Butha Buthe and soon had the opportunity to test the validity of his strategy. The repercussions of the mfecane had thrown the Hlubi across the Drankensberg front and dislodged the powerful Tlokwa under their queen regent, mma Ntatisi, and her son, Sikonyela. In their predatory migration, the Tlokwa attacked Butha Buthe on two occasions and were repulsed only with difficulty, carrying off Moshoeshoe's cattle and driving his people to the brink of starvation. It was clear that, although the principle of defense was found, a better site than Butha Buthe was needed, one where not only an army but the whole people could stand off attack indefinitely. When such a place was finally located about 1825,

Moshoeshoe led his people to the new site, called Thaba Bosiu, in a brilliantly executed march through bandit-and cannibal-infested territory. Now, at last he had a firm base on which to build a viable state. Although military defense was an essential element of Basotho policy, the success of the nation rested ultimately on the wisdom and diplomatic skills of Moshoeshoe himself, and Moshoeshoe's statesmanship in turn was based upon several major principles. In the first place the psychology of military defense and the need for survival argued for the primacy of peaceful negotiation over warfare. Again and again, Moshoeshoe resorted to diplomacy in place of force and, more often than not, his patience was rewarded.

To some extent these were elements of a negative posture of defense, the positive side of which was the creation of a healthy, strong Basotho nation. Here again Moshoeshoe successfully brought into play his diplomatic talents. Persuasion, not force, held the loyalty of the many different people who came to live in the mountain refuge with its center at Thaba Bosiu. Small heterogeneous groups were permitted to retain their own leaders under the surveillance of members of Moshoeshoe's ruling family. Larger groups were essentially self-governing, required only to acknowledge the ultimate authority of Moshoeshoe. Cultural differences were gradually overcome by propinquity, and national bonds grew strong in a spirit of mutual need and respect. Above all was the example of Moshoeshoe himself, always the man of peace, always the diplomat, always planning reason before choler. In the difficult days of the Boer expansion, Moshoeshoe was to be the salvation of the Basotho nation.

2.4.3. *Fang*

The Fang are especially known for their guardian figures which they attached to the wooden boxes containing bones of the ancestors. The bones, tradition, are said to contain the power of the dead person, in fact, the same amount of power that the person had while still alive.

The Fang mainly inhabit the hot, humid, equatorial rain forest of Gabon, making up 80% of the Gabonese population. They are of medium height and have a relatively powerful build and pride themselves greatly on their physical beauty.

The Fang are reported to have moved from the North East centuries ago and settled in the region to farm. Because they are a warrior like people they quickly conquered the native inhabitants. Many ethnic groups still fear the Fang because of their powerful aggressive tendencies. The Fang are also known for their older practice of cannibalism, which they practiced unashamedly during the 17th centuries and earlier. Using slash and burn techniques the Fang still farm as their chief occupation, though during the early years of European settlement many resorted to elephant ivory hunting to provide ivory to traders.

Leadership in Fang villages is inherited and the leader usually supposed to be descended from the family who started the village. The leader also serves as the spiritual leader, able to communicate with the ancestors of the village. He does this by the wearing of masks, which are also an important feature of Fang artwork.

2.5. Psychological analysis on African tribes

Tribes tend to fight a lot. Most tribes are agrarian, and there always are disputes over land and crime. Tribes don't have don't have the strong legal systems of kingdoms and nations, so justice is seen as a personal chore. Within tribes, there usually is a system of tribal elders who arbitrate these disputes. But when the disputes are between tribes, arbitration is difficult, usually impossible. Violence and endless blood feuds result.

Africa has the largest number of active tribes on the planet, over 500 at last count. The nations of Africa are artificial creations, put together by European colonial powers in the late 19th century. In the1950s and 60s, most of these colonies were given freedom. These new nations still had their tribes, plus poverty and weak legal systems. The colonial powers enforced peace, often with guns, but also with thousands of bureaucrats imported from Europe. After independence, most of these bureaucrats went home.

The tribal animosities began to emerge very quickly after independence. Most of these nations soon found themselves run by military dictators. It was very ugly, but it kept peace. However, unlike the colonial bureaucrats, the locals were far more corrupt, often because they were intent on taking care of their economy, as well as making most of the population increasingly angry over the poverty and injustice.

When democracy got its chance again in the late 1900s, it was because Africans realized that, alone in the world, their economies had been steadily shrinking through the 1980s. The end of cold war also eliminated the ability to play off the superpowers against one another, thus eliminating another source of income. They needed change, but democracy alone was not enough. With the generals replaced by the politicians, tribal violence is on the rise again. A good case is Nigeria, Africa's most populous nation. Nigeria has some 250 "ethnic group" (most organized as tribes around shared customs, language and culture) in a population of 122 million.

Pre-colonial warfare is returning. In the past, the various kingdoms that existed before the colonial period had ethnic minorities that were oppressed, and they have not forgotten. It's fashionable to blame all this on the European colonial governments, but the one Sub-Saharan nation that was not colonized, Ethiopia, also experiences frequent civil war and rebellion because of its dozen or so different ethnic groups.

No one has yet come up with a quick solution for this problem. Historically, the only thing that works is gradual absorption of many smaller groups into the larger ones. This has been going on more rapidly in the last few centuries, making it easier for many stable nations to form. Africans want to hold on to their colonial era borders, even if it means constant threat of unrest. This is preferable to the pre-colonial tribal warfare. But how do you keep the tribes from fighting?

Admitting there is a problem in the first step, and most African nations are doing that. They are stressing the need for national unity. But with corrupt police and civil servants, plus rampart poverty, too many people still have to fall back on the tribe for economic and judicial relief. History provides little comfort. Everywhere else, tribes only faded away after centuries of increasing prosperity and the development of honest and efficient government. Put more simply, the central government had to compete with the tribal organization to provide better living standards and legal systems. This works, it was working during the colonial period. But it only works long term if the locals themselves provide the judges, police, politicians and bureaucrats.

CHAPTER THREE
AGGRESSION: NATURE AND CAUSES

3.1. GENDER AND AGGRESSION

Gender is a factor that plays a role in both human and animal aggression. Males are historically believed to be generally more physically aggressive than females from an early age and men commit the vast majority of murders. This is one of the most robust and reliable behavioral sex differences, and it has been found across many different age groups and cultures. There is evidence that males are quicker to aggression and more likely than females to express their aggression physically. When considering indirect forms of non-violent aggression, such as relational aggression and social rejection, some scientists argue that females can be quite aggressive although female aggression is rarely expressed physically.

Studies show, that females in general have a better control over their emotions in comparison to males. Also, males are more likely to retaliate when provoked to gain recognition; females are more likely to retaliate in a violent way because they are shield by moral sense. Although females are likely to initiate physical violence, they can express aggression by using variety of non-physical means. Exactly which method women use to express aggression is something that varies from culture to culture.

3.2. Culture and aggression

Culture is a factor that plays a role in aggression. Tribal or band societies existing before or outside of modern states have sometimes been depicted as peaceful 'noble savages' or alternatively as brutish 'beasts'. The Kung Bushmen were described as 'the harmless people' in a popular work by Elizabeth Marshall Thomas in 1958.

Studies of hunter gathers show a range of different societies. In general, aggression, conflict and violence sometimes occur, but direct confrontation is generally avoided and conflict is socially managed by a variety of verbal and non-verbal methods. Different rates of aggression or violence, currently or in the past, within or between groups, have been linked to the structuring of societies and environmental conditions influencing factors such as resources or property acquisition, land and substance technique and population change. Analyzing aggression politically or culturally is complicated by the fact that the label 'aggressive' can itself be used as a way of asserting judgment from a particular point of view. Whether a coercive or violent method of social control is perceived as aggression-or as legitimate versus illegitimate aggression-depends on the position of the relevant parties in relation to the social order of their culture. This in turn can relate to factors such as; norms for coordinating actions and dividing resources; what is considered self-defense or provocation; attitudes towards 'outsiders', attitude towards specific groups such as women, the disabled or the lower status: the availability of alternative conflict resolution strategies and the likes.

3.3. Causal factors of aggression

Although specific causes of aggression are not known, some studies have shown that abnormal brain chemistry or structural changes may play a role. Environmental and genetic also seem to be involved. Aggression is potential symptoms of diseases, disorders or conditions that interfere with thought processes, such as dementia, post-traumatic, stress disorder, schizophrenia and number of personality disorders.

3.3.1. *Physiological factors*

Undoubtedly there are physiological factors at play in aggression. These factors play a huge role in what types of people will be predisposed to being aggressive. Biology alone, however, does not define the entirety of aggression. A person may be predisposed to be aggressive, but there are thousands of other factors in that person's environment that can be encouraged or detract from an aggressive behavior.

i. Testosterone

One biological factor that may be related to aggression in human males is testosterone level. Testosterone is a male sex hormone, which is responsible for many male bodily characteristics and which has been linked to aggression in monkeys. Recent studies suggest that in human as well higher levels of testosterone are associated with higher levels of aggression. One large-scale study involved more than 4400 male U.S veterans. The men were given various psychological tests, some of which tapped aggressiveness; they also had blood samples taken from them so that their testosterone level could be determined. Men who had higher levels of testosterone were more likely to have a history of aggression. Since aggressive behavior in males can sometimes lead to antisocial behavior, we might expect that high testosterone would be an impediment to success in human life.

These findings provide some evidence for a biological basis of aggression in humans, and hence for view that aggression is like a drive.

Still in these studies the link between testosterone and aggression is often tenuous-large numbers of subjects are needed to find the effect-which suggests the need to look elsewhere for determinants of aggression.

ii. *Alcohol*

Alcohol has been shown to increase aggression especially when provoked. Alcohol disinhibits an individual. This can be compared to the long-term disinhibits that occurs in individuals with antisocial behavior due to an underdeveloped prefrontal cortex. Over half of all acts of rape occur while the aggression is under the influence of alcohol.
Alcohol consumption may promote aggression because people expect it to. For example, research using real and mock beverages shows that people who believe they have consumed alcohol begin to act more aggressively, regardless of which beverage they actually consumed. Alcohol-related expectancies that promote male aggressiveness, combined with the widespread perception of intoxicated women as sexually receptive and less able to defend themselves, could account for the association between drinking and date rape.

3.3.2. *Environmental factors*

Social learning theory offers a perspective from which we can examine specific influences on aggression. Under what conditions do we aggress? What environmental influences pull our trigger?

i. Weather

An uncomfortable environment also heightens aggressive tendencies. Offensive odors, cigarette smoke, and air pollution have been linked with aggressive behavior . But the most studied environmental effects irritant is heat, William Griffitt found that compared with students who answered questionnaires in a room with a normal temperature, those who did so in an uncomfortably hot room (over 90 0f) reported feeling more tired and aggressive and expressed more hostility toward a stranger. Follow-up experiments revealed that heat also trigger retaliate actions.

ii. Crowding

CROWDING- the subjective feeling of not having enough space-is stressful. Crammed in the back of a bus, trapped in slow-moving free-way traffic, or living three to a small room in a college dorm diminishes one's sense of control. Might such experiences also heighten aggression? The stress experienced by animals allowed to overpopulate a confined environment does heighten aggressiveness. But it is a rather large leap from rats in an enclosure or deer on an island to humans in a city. Nevertheless, it's true that dense urban areas do experience higher rates of crime and emotional distress. Even when they don't suffer higher crime rates, residents of crowded cities may feel more fearful. Toronto's crime has been four times higher than Hong-Kong which is four times more densely populated-have reported feeling more fearful on their city's streets.

3.3.3. Psychological factors

Many psychological factors affect whether we behave aggressively in specific situations. From gang violence to rape and war, people may employ several types of self-justification to make it psychologically easier to harm other people. Aggressors may blame the victim for imagined wrongs or otherwise convince themselves that the victim "deserves it'. They may also dehumanize their victims, as the guard in the Stanford prison study did when he began to view the prisoners as "cattle".

i. *Frustration*

The frustration-aggression hypothesis was one of the first systematic theories that attempted to describe when a person would act aggressively. The theory proposed that all acts of aggression are due to frustration. Frustration is an aversive feeling that occurs when a person is blocked from achieving a goal. A more recent version of this theory suggests that frustration will only lead to aggression if it produces a negative emotion like anger.

A common belief about frustration is that it creates pent-up energy that must eventually be released. That is, even if a person does not act out the aggression immediately, the frustration will build up energy that must eventually come out. The release of unexpressed emotional energy was termed Catharsis by Freud. The concept of catharsis suggests that it may be possible to "get out" aggressive urges in a safer, more controlled manner (like hitting a punching bag or watching a violent movie). However, the research on this topic clearly shows that this prediction (and the general notion of catharsis0 is wrong. In fact, the research suggests that the opposite is true-acting aggressively (or even watching someone else act aggressively) usually leads to more aggressive.

ii. *Physical abuse*

The value of physical or corporal punishment is disputed among psychologists; some regard it as harmless while many others consider it potentially harmful. Some researchers have controversially suggested that parental use of physical punishment maybe causally related to the development of aggression. The nature of this relationship, however, has been hypothesized among various writers to be linear and curvilinear, positive and negative, and even nonexistent. What is lacking is detailed critical review of the literature examining physical punishment and its causal relationship to aggressive or violent behavior.

An examination of the literature reveals that most studies are supportive of a relationship between physical punishment and aggression. Further, prospective studies, suggests that physical punishment may contribute etiologically towards the development of aggressive behavior. Of those few studies which provided the relevant data, a majority favor a curvilinear, rather than a linear, causal relationship. However, the impact of physical punishment on children's aggression levels may vary with the age and gender of the child. The very few studies which examine physical punishment in interaction with other parental factors 9such as discussion and use of reasoning) suggests that any noxious effects of physical punishment may be mitigated by other parental disciplinary behaviors. Finally, however, this literature's conclusions are greatly limited by significant methodological flaws, notably control for factors such as child abuse, parental substance abuse, and other parenting behaviors.

3.4. Individual differences

Although it is clear that aggression can vary across cultures and genders, a different question is whether there is consistency in aggression within specific individuals, in other words, do some people simply tend to be more aggressive than others, across ages and situations? The evidence on this point is fairly clear: although situational variables, certainly do influence whether and how someone will aggress, there are some stable individual differences in aggressiveness. Aggression in childhood does predict aggression in adolescence and adulthood, along with adult criminality, alcohol abuse, and other antisocial behaviors.

What types of personalities tend to be associated with aggressiveness? Ann Bettencourt recently conducted a meta-analysis of sixty-three studies to answer this question. People tend to hold hostile cognition, express anger, and exhibit irritability tend to behave more aggressively. Other traits associated with aggression, however, tend to predict aggression reliably only under conditions of provocation-that is, situations that are perceived to be aversive or stressful. Among these traits are emotional susceptibility (tendency to feel distressed, inadequate, and vulnerable to perceived threats), narcissism (tendency to have an inflated sense of self-worth and self-love, but without a strong set of beliefs to support these feelings, thereby leaving the person's self-esteem unstable and sensitive to criticism), type A personality (tendency to be driven by feelings of inadequacy to try to prove oneself through personal accomplishments) and impulsivity (being relatively unable to control one's thoughts and behaviors). When provoked, individuals with these traits are not much more likely than others to behave aggressively. Provocation, however, can light the relatively short fuses of these individuals, leading to the potential explosion of aggression.

3.5. Learning that aggression is rewarding

Aggression may be a natural response to aversive events, but learning can alter natural reactions. Animals naturally eat when they are hungry. But if appropriately rewarded or pushed, they can be taught either to overeat or to starve.

Our reactions are more likely to be aggressive in situations where experience has taught us that aggression pays. Children whose aggression successfully intimidates other children may become more aggressive. Animals that have successfully fought to get food or mates become increasingly ferocious.

Different cultures model, reinforce, and evoke different tendencies toward violence. For example, crime rates are higher and average happiness is lower in countries marked by a great disparity between rich and power.

Social influence also appears in high violence rates among cultures and families that experience minimal father care. It is important, however, to note how many people are leading gentle, even heroic lives amid social stress, reminding us again that individuals differ. The person matters. That people differ over time and place reminds us that environment also differs, and situations matter. Yesterday's plundering Vikings have become today's peace-promoting Scandinavians. Like all behavior, aggression arises from the interaction of persons and situations.

3.6. The goals of aggressive behavior

Social psychological research suggests that aggressive behavior may serve a wide range of motivations, including the desire to influence other people, to gain power and dominance over others, to create an impression of toughness, to gain money or social approval, or simply to discharge negative feelings. Sigmund Freud suggests that aggressive behavior may serve as a goal in itself.

3.6.1.   *Instincts: drives toward death and destruction*

Freud's view of human motivation had originally included only "life instincts"-selfish drives that contributed to the individual's survival and reproduction. After viewing, the ravages of World War I, though, he added a 'death instincts'-an innate pull to end one's own life. Freud realized that a death instinct would conflict with the life instincts. So Freud postulated that rather than killing ourselves, we redirect our self-destructive instinct toward the destruction of other people.
In the past psychologists thought about an "aggressive instinct", they often assumed that the environment would not affect such an inner destructive drive. But although Lorenzo's evolutionary models of aggressive drive is like Freud's theory of "death instinct" in assuming an inherent tendency to be aggressive, it is different in presuming an interaction between drive and events in the environment. Human (including animals) will not be inclined to act aggressively unless the drive is triggered by something outside (such as threat, an attack, or a frustration).

3.6.2.   *Aggression and adaptive goals*

According to modern evolutionary analyses, humans are not "programmed" to be blindly aggressive. Aggressive behavior is one strategy for survival and reproduction, useful in some situations but not in most others. Across many different animal species, aggression has been found to serve a number of goals, allowing animals to control their territorial boundaries, to divide limited resources, and to defend their young. But any thoughtless tendency to commit random acts of aggression to let off steam would make little survival sense. Because aggression always bears the risk of retaliation and could result in injury or death, pure hostility vented in the absence of an immediate, useful goal would hurt an animal's chance to survive and reproduce.

This analysis suggests that aggressive behavior is never a goal in itself. Instead psychologists now assume that aggressive behavior is designed to serve some function. Because it may backfire and lead to injury and death for the perpetrator, psychologists also presume that people usually use aggressiveness only when other people avenues have failed.

CHAPTER FOUR
CONTROL OF AGGRESSION

4.1. Individual interventions

Treatment for aggression focuses on controlling it. People who behave aggressively should be seen by a qualified mental health professional. Early treatment is often helpful. Treatment focuses on helping people learn to control anger, express anger and frustration in a way that is appropriate, be responsible for their own actions, and learn to accept the consequences of their behavior. Problems in the family, at school and in the community also need to be addressed.

There are individual interventions to control aggression, which include Relaxation training, Self-control training, Communication skills training and Psychotherapy.

4.1.1. Relaxation training

This is the method which is effective in reducing tension and arousal states which often occur before aggressive behavior. People can use simple relaxation tools, like deep breathing to calm down. There are many different formal relaxation techniques. People can also follow these simple techniques:

– Breathe deeply from diaphragm (picture the breath coming up from the gut)

– Slowly repeat a calm word on phrase, like "relax", or "take it easy", which can be like a mantra, this while breathing deeply.

– Use imagery: see in your mind a relaxing experience. This can be an experience you have had or just one that you imagine.

– Do slow yoga-like exercises to relax your muscle and make you feel calmer.

People who display aggressive behavior should practice these techniques everyday so that they learn to use them without thinking about it when they are in a situation that is likely to make them aggressive.

4.1.2. Self-control training

There are several forms of self-control training, which teaches people to control their own anger and aggression by making verbal statements, in which the person tells him/herself to respond to anger and arousal by thinking first and then using less aggressive behavior. Self-control training includes rational restructuring, cognitive self-instruction, and stress inoculation. Self-control training has been proven to work and is being used more and more often.

4.1.3. Communication skills training

This method focuses on resolving conflicts by teaching people positive communication skills. It includes general communication training and negotiation training. To increase the chances that the agreements negotiated to resolve conflicts are lived up to, the aggressor and the person he/she behaved aggressively against draw up written agreements called behavioral contracts. This treatment is very promising in controlling aggression and reducing conflict between people.

4.1.4. Psychotherapy

Psychotherapy is a method of treating emotional problems in which the therapist and the patient work together to develop a supportive relationship. The Therapist encourages the patient to talk about his/her problems and to be optimistic that the therapy can help. He/she may suggest ways to cope with these problems. Techniques include psychoanalysis, group therapy, and behavioral therapy. It is not very effective in controlling aggression.

4.2. Group interventions

Group interventions to control aggression include psychological skill training, character education, values clarification, and moral education. They are typically done in small groups.

4.2.1. Psychological skill training

This method uses a series of psycho-educational procedures to teach people how to manage their aggression. These procedures include modeling, behavioral rehearsal, and feedback on performance. Psychological skill training has been demonstrated to be effective in controlling aggression.

4.2.2. Character education

It is a comprehensive series of lessons in pro-social character traits designed for use in elementary schools. It is usually done using the Character Education curriculum.

4.2.3. Values clarification

It tries to build pro-social values without indoctrination. It helps students develop, clarify, and apply their own values by freely and thoughtfully choosing among the alternatives. Research has shown that values clarification may work somewhat in decreasing destructive attitudes and behavior and in increasing constructive alternatives.

4.3. Anger management

Anger and aggression often, but not always, go hand in hand. Anger is a normal, and necessary, human emotions. It is how people naturally respond to threats, and it inspires powerful, often aggressive feelings that allow people to fight when they are attacked. When anger gets out of control, however, it becomes destructive and people respond aggressively. People need to express their anger. Doing this is an assertive, not aggressive, way is healthiest. Being assertive means that people make their needs clear and meet those needs without hurting others.

4.3.1. Calming

Another way of dealing with anger is that of trying to cool down and relax. This is particularly called for in cases of anger that is explosive, often this is even prior to self-analysis . Usually people with explosive anger think only after they have reacted, and by then it is regret, contrition or remorse that they feel and not anger. But it is important to remind ourselves often that our emotions influence but not control us unless we left them, and that if we desire hard enough to control them, we can. At a certain stage while your anger is rising you may become conscious of what is happening to you. This is the moment to act. Simple relaxation tools, such as deep breathing can help calm down angry feelings. There are books and courses that can teach relaxation techniques, and once learnt these techniques can be called upon in any situation.

4.3.2. Manual work

Some people may be helped to calm down by engaging in some strenuous exercise, such a splitting fire wood, gardening, jogging, or some other physical exercise. The rationale behind is that anger is energy, and like all energy, it can be transformed into some other form of energy. Therapists often use such techniques as requiring the client to hit a pillow, wring a towel or throw stones in a lake, thus venting out pent-up anger in a safe environment.

Sometimes circumstances do not permit one to immense oneself into physical work. You may be engaged in an office or on a journey or in a meeting. You cannot get out and mow the lawn or split firewood. But when circumstances permit it, it is good practice when you are angry to put your energy and mind to some hard work, and keep at it until you are quite exhausted. The likelihood is that you will find yourself in a better position to deal with the engaging situation more reasonably. At the same time you have the bonus of work accomplished. If you can avoid it, in a state of enragement keep away from work that requires intensive mental activity. Often you might end up messing things and increasing frustration at the same time.

Manual work doesn't always have to be such as creates perspiration and brings blister. You can file the papers or wash handkerchiefs. An untidy work environment itself is enough to increase it not generate anger. You are more likely to book for and fail to find things you need.

It is to be noted that calming and relaxation techniques may offer some temporary means of dealing with anger in order to bring it to manageable proportions. They are not a substitute to dealing with the issues which are the cause of one's anger. If a lazy student is angry at self for neglecting work that has to be done, no amount of wringing the towel or breathing techniques will take away the cause for the anger. The situation has to be confronted squarely.

4.4. Reducing aggression

We have examined instinct, frustration-aggression, and social learning theories of aggression, and we have scrutinized influences on aggression. How, then, can we reduce aggression? Do theory and research suggest ways to control aggression?

4.4.1. Cathartic model

"Youngsters should be taught to vent their anger", so advised Ann Landers. If a person "bottles up his rage, we have to find out an outlet, we have to give him an opportunity of letting off steam". So asserted the prominent psychiatrist Fritz Perls, "some expression of prejudice…lets of steam…it can siphon off conflict through words, rather than actions", so argued Andrew Sullivan . Articles on hate crimes, such statements assume the "hydraulic model" accumulated aggressive energy, like dammed-up water, needs a release.

The concept of Catharsis is usually credited to Aristotle. Although Aristotle actually said nothing about aggression, he did argue that we can purge emotions by experiencing them and that viewing the classic tragedies therefore enabled a CATHARSIS '(purgation') of pity and fear. To have an emotion executed, he believed, is to have that emotion released. The catharsis hypothesis has been extended to include the emotional release supposedly obtained not only by observing drama but also through recalling and revealing past event, through expressing emotions, and through various actions.

In laboratory tests of catharsis, Bushmen Brad invited angered participants to hit a punching bag while either ruminating about the person who angered them or thinking about becoming physically fit. A third group did not hit the punching bag. Then, when a chance to administer loud blasts of noise to the who angered them, people in the punching back plus rumination condition felt angrier and here most aggressive. Doing nothing at all more effectively reduced aggression than "blowing off steam".

4.4.2.   Social learning approach

If aggressive behavior is learned, then there is hope for its control. Let us briefly review factors that influence aggression and speculate how to counteract them. Aversive experiences such as frustrated expectations and personal attacks predispose hostile aggression. So it is wise to refrain from planting false, unreachable expectation in people's minds. Anticipated rewards and costs influence instrumental aggression. This suggests that we should reward cooperative, nonaggressive behavior. In experiments, children become less aggressive when caregivers ignore their aggressive behavior and reinforce their nonaggressive behavior. Moreover, there are limits to punishment's effectiveness. Most mortal aggression is impulsive, hot aggression-the result of an argument, and insult, or an attack. Thus, we must prevent aggression before it happens. We must teach nonaggressive conflict-resolution strategies. If mortal aggression were cool and instrumental we could hope that waiting till it happens and severely punishing the criminal afterward would deter such acts. In that world, states that impose the death penalty might have a lower murder rate than states without the death penalty. But in our world of hot homicide, that is not so.

To foster a gentle world, we could model and reward sensitivity and cooperation from an early age, perhaps by training parents how to discipline without violence. Training programs encourage parents to reinforce desirable behaviors and to frame statements positively ("when you finish cleaning your room you can go play", rather than, "if you don't clean your room, you're grounded"). One "aggression-replacement program" has reduced re-arrest rates of juvenile offenders and gang members by teaching to control anger, and raising their level of moral reasoning. Suggestions such as these can help us minimize aggression. But given the complexity of aggression's causes and the difficulty of controlling them, who can feel the optimism expressed by Andrew Carnegie's forecast that, in the twentieth century, " to kill a man will be considered as disgusting as we in this day consider it disgusting to eat one". Since Carnegie uttered those words in 1900, some 200 million human beings have been killed. It is a sad irony that although today we understand human aggression better than ever before, humanity's inhumanity endures. Nevertheless cultures can change. "The Vikings slaughtered end plundered," notes Natalie Angier. "Their descendants in Sweden haven't fought a war in nearly 200 years".

4.5. Reducing violence

4.5.1.   Media effects

The media, of course, play an important role in legitimizing-even glorifying-violence. What, then, can we do about it? Government censorship is one answer, but it is not a very popular one, for a number of reasons. Another alternative is to use public pressure to increase media self-censorship. Of course, the most powerful kind of public pressure would be a commercial boy-court. If violence did not sell, the media would not produce it. Unfortunately, however, violence continues to be a moneymaker. At this point education may well be the most effective approach. For example, treatment programs have been developed to curb children' undesirable reactions to T.V. these programs recommend that parent select shows that provide compelling, vivid pro-social models for their children. Researches on the effects of pro-social television are encouraging in this regard, this research suggests that pro-social TV programs produce stronger effects on behavior than do antisocial TV programs. Parents have also been advised to watch television with their children and to teach them how TV differs from real life, how imitating TV characters can produce undesirable outcomes, and how children might be harmed by watching TV. This kind of ongoing parental tutorial takes significant time and effort. But given the extent of media depictions of violence in our society, strengthening children's critical viewing skills is a wise investment.

The question of what to do about the potentially harmful effects of pornography leads to the same options described for depictions of nonsexual violence. Should pornography be banned? Should consumers be educated? Banning pornography raises a number of philosophical, political, and practical concerns. In addition, banning explicit sexual material would not prevent dehumanizing portrayals of women as sex objects or titillating but fully clothed scenes of rape, and sexual assault.

4.5.2. *Intimate violence*

Sex-education programs that emphasize the desirability of being respectful and considerate toward one's sexual partner, in addition to rape awareness programs that debunk various rape myths and increase sensitivity can be important tools in the effort to reduce sexual aggression. Many college campuses experience persistent problems with alcohol abuse, which can be a key factor in many rapes and other forms of sexual aggression. Preventing and treating alcohol abuse, therefore, can make for healthier, safer campuses.

Family violence, too, is a matter of grave societal concerns: and, because it is caused by multiple factors, it must be addressed by a variety of approaches. Laws and programs that protect victims of abuse and reduce the likelihood of continued violence abuse are vitally important. For example Peter Sicheldothom and John Heron concluded recently "the association between poverty and child maltreatment is one of the most consistent observations. Thus protecting families from violence also requires providing family members with educational and employment opportunities. Furthermore, because abuse of alcohol and other drugs so often leads to family violence, better education about the effects of such substances, as well as support for individuals who need help dealing with them, would be a worthy investment not only for these individuals but also for the people around them."

Ultimately, effective communication is the key to reducing intimate violence. Jealousy and distrust contribute too much of the violence that occurs between intimate partners. Insensitivities to others needs and fears, as well as acceptance of myths about rape, play important roles in sexual aggression. And children who grow up in abusive homes may learn aggressive scripts that teach them that the best way to respond to social problems is through aggression. Better communication can help address all these problems.

CONCLUSION

Throughout the history man has been selfish and individualistic, because of his egoistic tendency man tried to accumulate the necessary and unnecessary resources in order for survival. Because of this aggressiveness behavior, aggression was passed down from one generation to the other. Aggression has been a major problem affecting all human beings since the beginning of civilization to today. The worst part of it is that this day is found in all spheres of angels, in religious perspective, political, economical as well as in everyday life.

The difficult of defining aggression lie in the fact that there are many different kinds of aggressive behavior. Animal aggression has obvious parallels to the aggressive behavior exhibited by humans. Which type of behavior that will exhibited therefore depends on the environmental circumstances, the active neural circuits and the specific 'triggering' stimuli and/or how useful the behavior is to the animal/human exhibiting the aggression. All of these factors should therefore be considered when attempting to explain aggressive behavior-it is not enough to simply say he/she is aggressive or that tribe, society or community is aggressive.

In chapter two, one may note that the aggressive behavior which is found among the selected tribes differs based on the perception of morality as well as the sense of humanity. Hence it is through these tribes that we were able to pinpoint out and to understand how the Africans behave in a certain way. It was found out that some nations or tribes express their aggressive behavior not for injuring intentionally, but they do it for their common good. To live in peace and harmony while some they do it as a hobby to see other people suffering and for them to be respected and be fearful.

Human beings are not inherently violent, rapacious animals bent on brutality and self-destruction. Aggression is rather a result of repulsive cultural and political environment that conspire to frustrate and degrade our humanity. Aggression may never be eliminated entirely, but it can be reduced to very low levels by creating societies of freedom, self-awareness and compassion.

BIBLIOGRAPHY

ANDREA, A.J., Encyclopedia of the Crusades, Westport: Greenwood Press, 2003.

ALTEMEYER, B., The Authoritarian Spector, Cambridge: Harvard University Press, 1996.

ATKINSON, R.L., – ATKINSON, R.C., – SMITH, E.E., Introduction to Psychology, Philadelphia: Harcourt Brace College Publishers, 1993.

BANDURA, A., – EMILLIO, R., Analysis of Delinquency and Aggression, New York: Lawrence Erlbaum Associates, INC., 1976.

BANDURA, A., Aggression: A social learning Analysis, Engelwood Cliffs: Prentice-Hall, 1973.

BERKOWITZ, L., Aggression, New York: Mcgraw-Hill, 1993.

BERKOWITZ, L., Aggression: Its causes, consequences, and control, New York: Mcgraw-Hill, 1993.

BERK, D.E., – COWAN, C., Value Systems: Values as Systems in Turbulence and changes, Texas: The National Values Centre, 1992.

BUTCHER, S.H., Aristotle's theory of poetry and fine art, New York: Dover, 1951.

COSTANZO, M., Just Revenge, New York: St. Martin's, 1998.

DOUGLAS, T.K., – NEUBERG, S.L., – CIALDINI, R.B., Social Psychology, Boston: Pearson Education, INC, 2007.

FLETCHER, R., The Cross and the Crescent: Christianity and Islam from Muhammad to the Reformation, New York: Vikings, 2003.

GARLAKE, P., The Kingdoms of Africa, New York: Peter Bedrick Books, 1990.

HAMILTON, B., The Crusades, United Kingdom: Sutton Publishers, 1998.

KASSIN, S., – FEIN, S., – MARKUS, H.R., Social Psychology, Belmont: Cengage Learning, 2008.

KYAMBADDE, S.P., In God's own Image: Personal growth and Basic counseling skill, Nairobi: Pauline Publications Africa, 2007.

MYER, D.G., Exploring Psychology, New York: Worth Publishers, 2008.

MYER, D.G., Exploring Social Psychology, Boston: McGraw-Hill, 2007.

OSKAMP, S., – SCHULTZ, W., Social Psychology: An applied Perspective, New Jersey: Prentice-Hall, 2000.

ROBERT, W.J., A History of the African people, Illinois: Waveland Press, INC, 1998.

SIGMUND, F., Beyond the pleasure principle, trans. HUBBACK, C.J.M., London: Hogarth Press, 1953.

THOMAS, E.M., The Harmless people, New York: Vintage Books, 1958.

http://www.aggressivechristianity.net/islam/is-sword.htm, 19/07/2012

http://www.framentsweb.org/../innatetx.html, 16/07/2012.

http://appsychtextbk.wikispaces.com/prehistoric+aggression, 25/07/2012

http://www.the-highway.com/catholic2_Armstrong.html, 31/07/2012

http://www.wisegeek.com/what-is-a-war-of-aggression.htm, 23/07/2012 http://www.bachelorandmasters.com/critical, 23/07/2012

http://www.lewrockwell.com/barnett/barnett30.1.html, 31/07/2012

http://www.africaguide.com/culture/tribes/fang.htm, 30/07/2012

http://www.strategypage.com/dis/articles2001/20010924.asp, 24/07/2012

http://www.africaguide.com/culture/tribes/fang.htm, 30/07/2012

http://nazaggression.tripod.com/social.html, 27/07/2012

http://www.fags.org>fags.org>health, 10/07/2012